Find a Book!

By SHANNON MCCLINTOCK MILLER
Illustrations by KATHRYN DURST
Music by EMILY ARROW

CANTATA
LEARNING

WWW.CANTATALEARNING.COM

CANTATA LEARNING

Published by Cantata Learning
1710 Roe Crest Drive
North Mankato, MN 56003
www.cantatalearning.com

Library of Congress Cataloging-in-Publication Data
Names: Miller, Shannon (Shannon McClintock), author. | Durst, Kathryn,
 illustrator. | Arrow, Emily, composer.
Title: Find a book! / by Shannon McClintock Miller ; illustrations by Kathryn
 Durst ; music by Emily Arrow.
Description: North Mankato, MN : Cantata Learning, [2018] | Series: Library
 skills | Includes bibliographical references.
Identifiers: LCCN 2017004502 (print) | LCCN 2017017931 (ebook) | ISBN
 9781684100286 | ISBN 9781684100279 (hardcover : alk. paper)
Subjects: LCSH: Libraries--Juvenile literature. | Libraries--Songs and music.
 | Books and reading--Juvenile literature. | Books and reading--Songs and
 music. | Children's songs, English--United States--Texts.
Classification: LCC Z665.5 (ebook) | LCC Z665.5 .M55 2018 (print) | DDC
 027--dc23
LC record available at https://lccn.loc.gov/2017004502

Book design, Tim Palin Creative
Editorial direction, Flat Sole Studio
Executive musical production and direction, Elizabeth Draper
Music arranged and produced by Emily Arrow

Printed in the United States of America in North Mankato, Minnesota.
072017   0367CGF17

ACCESS THE MUSIC!
SCAN CODE WITH MOBILE APP
CANTATALEARNING.COM

TIPS TO SUPPORT LITERACY AT HOME

WHY READING AND SINGING WITH YOUR CHILD IS SO IMPORTANT

Daily reading with your child leads to increased academic achievement. Music and songs, specifically rhyming songs, are a fun and easy way to build early literacy and language development. Music skills correlate significantly with both phonological awareness and reading development. Singing helps build vocabulary and speech development. And reading and appreciating music together is a wonderful way to strengthen your relationship.

READ AND SING EVERY DAY!

TIPS FOR USING CANTATA LEARNING BOOKS AND SONGS DURING YOUR DAILY STORY TIME

1. As you sing and read, point out the different words on the page that rhyme. Suggest other words that rhyme.

2. Memorize simple rhymes such as Itsy Bitsy Spider and sing them together. This encourages comprehension skills and early literacy skills.

3. Use the questions in the back of each book to guide your singing and storytelling.

4. Read the included sheet music with your child while you listen to the song. How do the music notes correlate to the words of the song?

5. Sing along on the go and at home. Access music by scanning the QR code on each Cantata book. You can also stream or download the music for free to your computer, smartphone, or mobile device.

Devoting time to daily reading shows that you are available for your child. Together, you are building language, literacy, and listening skills.

Have fun reading and singing!

The library is a big place, and there are lots of books on all of the shelves. How will you find the book you want? Just look around. Your librarian has provided **clues** that will help you.

Now turn the page to learn how to find a book in the library. Remember to sing along!

Find a book!

A library full of books and fun
is a place where your mind can run.

Use these tips to help yourself
find a new book on the shelf.

FICTION

NON-
FICTION

PICTURE
BOOKS

8

Find a book!

The first thing you do is follow the signs.
These shelf markers can save you time!

Your librarian left you lots of clues.
Look for words and for pictures too.

GRAPHIC NOVELS

MAG

Find a book!

A library full of books and fun
is a place where your mind can run.

Use these tips to help yourself
find a new book on the shelf.

GRAPHIC NOVELS

Find a book!

Do you love racecars, horses, or space?
Search words can make a perfect **base**!

Keywords can give you some handy clues
for finding a book both cool and true.

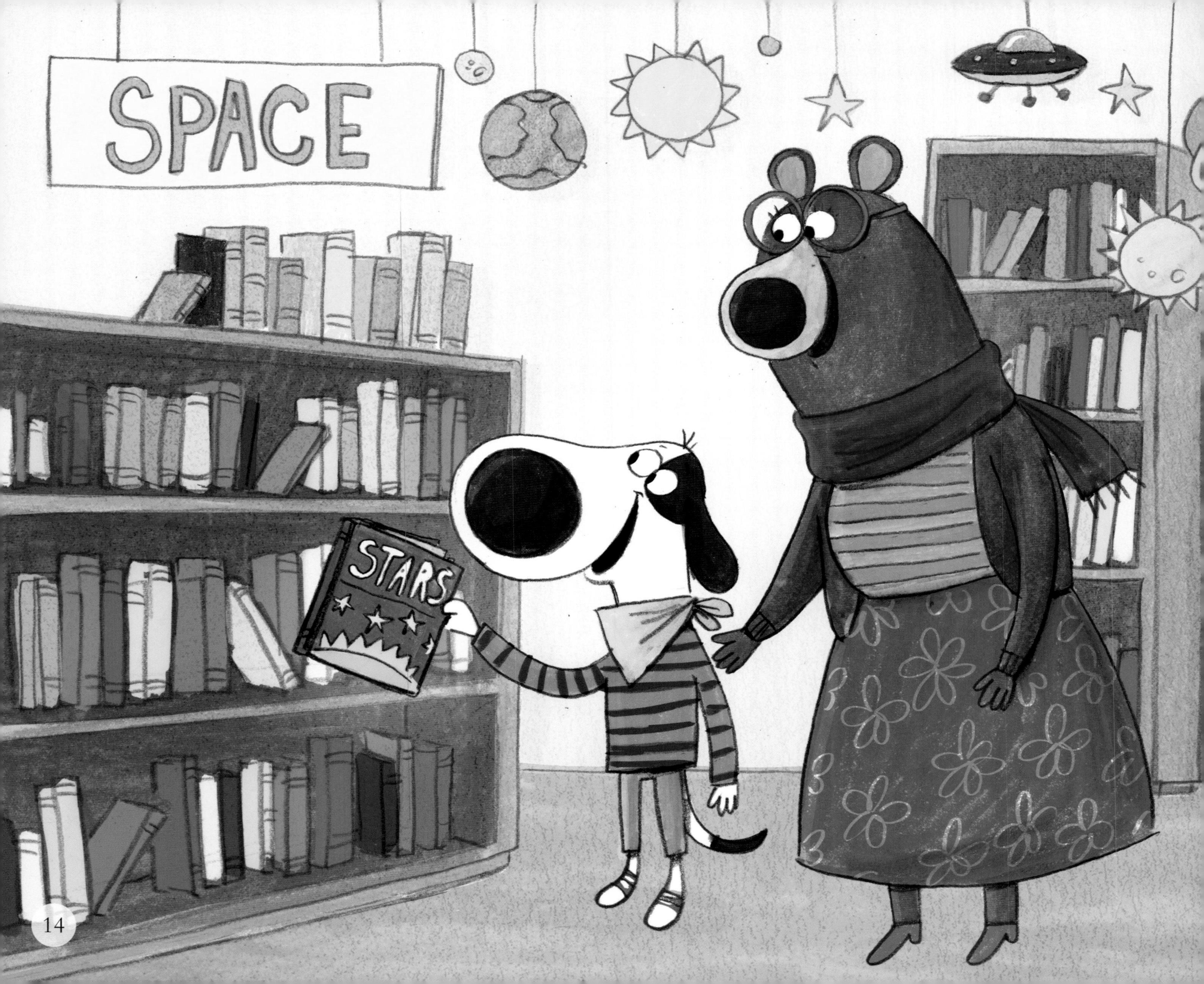
SPACE
STARS

Find a book!

A library full of books and fun
is a place where your mind can run.

Use these tips to help yourself
find a new book on the shelf.

Find a book!

Call numbers bring some books together.
The 500s take you all the way to the weather!

Find where a favorite book might be
by using the **Deweys** that you see.

Find a book!

Think of author and illustrator names.
Look for their books. Make it into a game!

Follow these leads to a favorite new book.
You can find one if you know how to look!

Find a book!

A library full of books and fun
is a place where your mind can run.

Use these tips to help yourself
find a new book on the shelf.

Now choose a book and a comfy chair
because reading can take you anywhere!

SONG LYRICS
Find a Book!

Find a book!
A library full of books and fun
is a place where your mind can run.
Use these tips to help yourself
find a new book on the shelf.

Find a book!
The first thing you do is follow the signs.
These shelf markers can save you time!
Your librarian left you lots of clues.
Look for words and for pictures too.

Find a book!
A library full of books and fun
is a place where your mind can run.
Use these tips to help yourself
find a new book on the shelf.

Find a book!
Do you love racecars, horses, or space?
Search words can make a perfect base!
Keywords can give you some handy clues
for finding a book both cool and true.

Find a book!

A library full of books and fun
is a place where your mind can run.
Use these tips to help yourself
find a new book on the shelf.

Find a book!
Call numbers bring some books together.
The 500s take you all the way to the weather!
Find where a favorite book might be
by using the Deweys that you see.

Find a book!
Think of author and illustrator names.
Look for their books. Make it into a game!
Follow these leads to a favorite new book.
You can find one if you know how to look!

Find a book!
A library full of books and fun
is a place where your mind can run.
Use these tips to help yourself
find a new book on the shelf.

Now choose a book and a comfy chair
because reading can take you anywhere!

Find a Book!

Kindie
Emily Arrow

Chorus

Find a book! A library full of books and fun is a place where your mind can run. Use these tips to help yourself find a new book on the shelf.

Verse

1. Find a book! The first thing you do is follow the signs. These shelf markers can save you time! Your librarian left you lots of clues. Look for words and for pictures too.

Interlude

Chorus

Verse 2
Find a book!
Do you love racecars, horses, or space?
Search words can make a perfect base!
Keywords can give you some handy clues
for finding a book both cool and true.

Interlude

Chorus

Verse 3
Find a book!
Call numbers bring some books together.
The 500s take you all the way to the weather!
Find where a favorite book might be
by using the Deweys that you see.

Interlude

Bridge

Find a book! Think of author and illustrator names. Look for their books. Make it into a game! Follow these leads to a favorite new book. You can find one if you know how to look!

Interlude

Outro

Find a book! A library full of books and fun is a place where your mind can run. Use these tips to help yourself find a new book on the shelf. Now choose a book and a comfy chair because reading can take you anywhere!

GLOSSARY

base—the lowest part or start of something

call numbers—numbers on the spines of books that tell which section of the library a book is located

clues—something that helps a person find something or understand something

Deweys—numbers in the Dewey decimal system; a book's Dewey tells which section of the library a book is located

keywords—important words used to search for something

GUIDED READING ACTIVITIES

1. Have you ever looked for a book in the library? Did you use any of the clues mentioned in this book? If yes, which ones?

2. Next time you visit the library, use one of the clues in this book to help you find a book.

3. What types of books do you like to read? What is your favorite book? What is it about? Tell someone in your class why you like the book.

TO LEARN MORE

Becker, Bonny. *A Library Book for Bear*. Sommerville, MA: Candlewick Press, 2014.

Gassman, Julie. *Do Not Bring Your Dragon to the Library*. North Mankato, MN: Capstone, 2016.

Rissman, Rebecca. *Going to a Library*. North Mankato, MN: Heinemann-Raintree, 2012.

Rustad, Martha E. H. *Let's Go to the Library*. North Mankato, MN: Capstone, 2013.